At its worst, the choice debate is partisan, shedding more heat than light on the subject. Pitting ideologues on both sides of the question against each other, it is more reminiscent of a political campaign... than a discussion of education policy.

—National Working Commission on Choice in K-12 Education

TABLE OF CONTENTS

EXECUTIVE SUMMARY

Although "choice" is often discussed as something novel in public education, a variety of options have long existed in American schools. From magnet, alternative, and charter schools through homeschooling and recent judicial acceptance of regulated vouchers, today's public school system provides a growing number of educational options for families. The discussion about "choice" today is as much about "how" and "how much" as it is about "whether."

Role and Work of the Commission

The National Working Commission on Choice in K-12 Education was established to explore how choice works and to examine how communities interested in the potential benefits of new school options could obtain them while avoiding choice's potential damage. The Commission was not created as an advocate for choice or to make judgments about whether school choice is desirable or undesirable.

In going about its work, the Commission reviewed the possible effects of choice in light of the core value of public education, that all children should be thoroughly educated, so that they may pursue their own dreams and contribute to a democratic, egalitarian, and prosperous American society. Drawing from that value, the Commission explored choice in terms of four key issues: benefits to children whose parents choose new schools; benefits to children whose families do not exercise choice; effects on the national commitment to equal opportunity and school desegregation; and advancement of social cohesion and common democratic values.

Analysis of How Choice Works

A growing body of research exists on the links between choice and those four outcomes. Although much of the research is rigorous and informative, it falls short of providing definitive guidance on how choice will work in every case. The Commission, therefore, tried to open up the "black box" of choice, the set of events that must occur if choice is to have results, whether positive or negative. We identified a number of key factors that link choice with outcomes. Policy and investment factors include student targeting, funding, performance measurement, parent information, student access to schools, regulation, and accountability. Individual behavior factors include parents' preferences, student effort, school options, and teacher response.

Because so much depends on how these factors are combined and interrelate, choice is unlikely to be the panacea for American schools trumpeted by its advocates. It is equally unlikely to be the death of public support for American education, the fear of its detractors. There is nothing automatic about choice. The links between choice and its outcomes are not so mechanical that outcomes can be totally controlled or perfectly predicted. Choice's outcomes, for good or ill, depend heavily on how communities structure and implement it.

In education policy, just as in business, there is no free lunch. In the design of choice programs it is possible to preserve some values, like close supervision of schools, only by trading off others, such as creation of new options. Similarly, it is possible to limit the amount of public funds that move with children as their parents choose alternative schools, but only at the expense of more ambitious options and innovation.

Figure 1 displays the "no free lunch" message graphically. It illustrates how the intersection of two different areas of policy—prescription versus

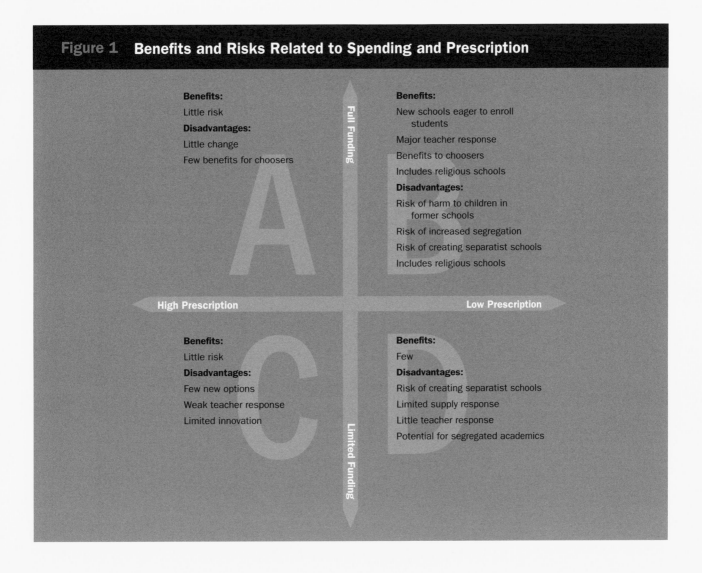

Figure 1 Benefits and Risks Related to Spending and Prescription

Full Funding

Benefits:
Little risk

Disadvantages:
Little change
Few benefits for choosers

Benefits:
New schools eager to enroll students
Major teacher response
Benefits to choosers
Includes religious schools

Disadvantages:
Risk of harm to children in former schools
Risk of increased segregation
Risk of creating separatist schools
Includes religious schools

High Prescription ← → **Low Prescription**

Benefits:
Little risk

Disadvantages:
Few new options
Weak teacher response
Limited innovation

Benefits:
Few

Disadvantages:
Risk of creating separatist schools
Limited supply response
Little teacher response
Potential for segregated academics

Limited Funding

flexibility and generous funding of options versus limited funding—creates four separate quadrants. Each of the four represents a different reality.

What is clear immediately from Figure 1 is that communities that regulate new schools tightly are likely to get few options, even if they provide relatively generous funding. The major benefit of tight regulation is that these communities risk little; the major disadvantage is that they gain very few new options.

Generous funding is the way to provide more choice, but here communities will have to worry about managing risk. Communities that provide full funding and little regulation will have to watch for potential negative results, including the possibility of increased segregation. Communities intent on avoiding such results could move in the direction of greater prescription—for example, by adopting arrangements like chartering that allow public agencies to screen potential school providers in advance and hold schools accountable for performance.

In addition to these risks, expanding choice opens up legal and philosophical issues involving support for religious schools. While research can shed some light on these questions, in the end they are questions of law and social philosophy.

Designing Options to Achieve Particular Results

What is clear is that state and local leaders considering choice face important decisions about how to fund and oversee choice. The Commission learned important lessons about how communities can design and manage choice to achieve particular outcomes and avoid others. For example:

Promoting learning for children whose families choose. School performance measurement and parent information are necessary for parents to make good choices. At the same time, if providers of schools available for choice are to offer high-quality programs, they need to receive per-pupil funding comparable to that of district-managed schools and have the freedom both to hire teachers on the basis of school fit and to attract students and parents on the basis of their distinctive offerings. If disadvantaged children are to benefit, their parents need to be given the first opportunity to choose, and schools need to accept public funding as full payment for tuition.

Protecting learning for children of parents who are slow to choose.
Communities that want to protect children who remain in district schools
would make sure that schools threatened by competition get at least the same
real per-dollar funding as other district-run schools, and are free to hire teachers, set pay for staff with rare or critical skills, and make tradeoffs between
salaries and purchase of new methods and materials.

Avoiding segregation. Communities that want to make sure choice does
not lead to greater segregation would take all the actions listed above. In addition, these communities would conduct or oversee scrupulously fair admissions processes for all schools, including lotteries for schools that are oversubscribed. These communities would also need to withdraw public funding from
schools that target poor or minority students for discipline or expulsion.

Avoiding harm to social cohesion. Communities that want to ensure
that choice does not lead to the establishment of schools that teach hatred or
discrimination or stratify students by income, class, or race need to do everything listed above. Communities concerned about civic cohesion might also
require teaching of core civics courses emphasizing the values of equality,
democracy, tolerance, and Constitutional principles of equality and freedom
of speech. These communities would, in addition, create incentives for effective civics-oriented teaching by measuring student attitudes and reporting
results on school exit exams. Clearly, communities need to approach this
topic with the recognition that prescriptions that look desirable to some may
look capricious to others.

Phasing in Choice

There is no way a community can establish all the "right" policies and
make all the "right" decisions and investments in advance. Saying "we

can't try choice until all the questions are answered" is equivalent to saying "we will never try it." In implementing choice, state and community leaders, elected officials, and philanthropists can play important roles.

Elected officials need to build several capacities that state governments and school districts now lack. In addition to allocating funds on a per-pupil basis, providing good school performance information, and running fair admissions lotteries, government needs to create an environment of fair competition and reliable rules so that both alternative and district-run schools have a chance to offer effective instruction.

Foundations and the federal government can also contribute to the sensible design and implementation of choice programs. Philanthropy's potential role can be significant: in sponsoring planning for choice, developing the capacities of schools and educators, and providing a "watchdog" function, ensuring that someone complains if choice programs are not implemented as planned. The federal government can facilitate the transition by allowing categorical program funds to follow children to new schools of choice and by investing in national research on how choice works.

Choice programs will not be implemented easily or even cheaply. The surest way to help guarantee their success will be conscious, well-thought-out strategies drawing on the best thinking of the worlds of government and philanthropy. And perhaps the surest way to encourage their failure is to implement choice programs quickly, carelessly, and cheaply, optimistic that at some point things will all work out for the best.

PREFACE

Although in recent years "choice" has been debated as something novel in public education, a variety of options have long existed in American schools. In fact, a fully functioning system of vouchers and choice was established in American higher education about 50 years ago. In public schools, families with the means have always been able to live in neighborhoods served by the schools they want or pay private school tuition. Whether or not one accepts the wisdom and desirability of "choice" in K-12 education, the recent growth of alternative schools, charter schools, homeschooling, educational options via the Internet, and judicial acceptance of vouchers has dramatically expanded the options available to American parents for the education of their children.

Recognizing that choice in some form is here to stay and will likely expand in the near future, the Bill & Melinda Gates Foundation and the Annie E. Casey Foundation agreed in 2001 to support the establishment of a National Working Commission on Choice in K-12 Education. This was to be a "working commission." That is to say, it was not established to enter contentious ideological debates, to render a final judgment on whether choice is good or bad, or even to calculate a total score based on the plusses and minuses of existing choice programs. Rather, the group was asked to look closely at positive and negative possible outcomes of choice and suggest how communities that want to get the potential benefits might do so while avoiding choice's potential harms. Faced with the likelihood that parents will be offered more schooling options, the Commission was also asked to explain how choice might work, to assess both risks and benefits to children and important civic values, and to suggest how choice programs might best be designed.

The Commission hoped to explain choice so that state and local leaders, educators, philanthropists, and citizens could better understand how to balance its benefits and risks. It was housed and staffed at The Brookings Institution's Brown Center on Education Policy. Commission members were selected for their expertise and to represent a spectrum of analytical approaches and views about choice. All have published books or articles on the subject. Some are sanguine about choice's possible benefits; others are skeptical. All agree that choice is one among many possible means of providing public education, and that all possible means, including those commonly in use, are neither inherently good nor bad in themselves. Structures for providing public education are good to the degree they enable all children to learn what they need to know to become self-reliant, capable, and public-spirited citizens. They are bad to the extent that they fail to provide effective education for all children.

The members of this commission accepted a common frame of reference, an assumption that "choice" does not educate anyone. Choice is not a teacher, a classroom, or an instructional resource. If choice affects what students learn, it works indirectly, by leading to changes in what students experience, read, and hear. The same is true about other possible outcomes of choice. Choice forms only part of an institutional framework in which particular events can occur.

Starting from that assumption, Commission members set out to open up the "black box" of this framework—the complex linkages connecting choice and important potential outcomes, good and bad.[1] So, for example, Commission members found themselves sketching out the chain of events that must occur if children whose families exercise choice are to learn more than they would have learned in the school to which their district assigned them. Other Commission members sketched out other sequences of events that might be set in motion by choice. Some of these sequences could lead to desirable outcomes—for instance, school improvement throughout a local community, even for children whose parents ignore the option to choose. Some could lead to unmistakably undesirable outcomes, such as increased segmentation of children by income and social class or segregation by race.

As we went about our work, we became convinced that the ideological fervor and conviction of those on each side of the debate mask a great deal of uncertainty. Each side has asserted that particular outcomes of choice are certain to occur. However, as we soon learned, results good and bad depend on many things. The effects, far from being inevitable, depend on how choice programs are implemented. Here as elsewhere, when scholars jump to conclusions they mislead the public.

The very word "choice" has become an important symbol as contending sides define it to gain advantage. Thus, some choice advocates characterize choice as nothing more than restoring parental rights, while some opponents characterize it as turning a sacred public trust over to unregulated market forces. The Commission is determined to restore "choice" to its proper status as a neutral word than can be used in reasoned public discourse. The Commission defines the term more fully in the body of this document. The basic definition is any arrangement that gives parents options among schools. With appropriate modifiers the word "choice" can refer to a public school district program that allows parents to choose among existing schools; to a state program that charters a large number of new schools among which parents are free to choose; or to an unrestricted market in which government pays tuition in any school a family chooses. The question of whether "choice" is a good thing has no single answer. Since the response depends on how choice is designed, the answer can vary from one design to another. The Commission has drawn from many sources—American K-12 experience, other countries' experience, American experience with options in higher education, and research on choice in other areas of public policy. Although much of this evidence is mixed and incomplete, all of it illuminated our thinking.

On a personal note, I want to thank my colleagues on the Commission for their hard work and commitment to this effort. Although each would undoubtedly produce a slightly different document, all support the broad directions outlined here.

Paul T. Hill

PAUL T. HILL (CHAIR)
Director, Center on Reinventing Public Education
Daniel J. Evans School of Public Affairs
University of Washington

Part 1

OPTIONS IN EDUCATION

AMERICAN PUBLIC EDUCATION IN THE 21ST CENTURY IS FAR from the monolithic, one-size-fits-all system that its critics deride and some public school advocates find themselves defending. The scale and speed with which options have been expanded is surprising. Ten years ago, for example, charter schools and homeschooling were suspicious new developments that would surely go nowhere. Today, school districts like Chicago and Cleveland use school chartering as part of their efforts to improve education for disadvantaged students, and six states fund vouchers to allow some students to attend private schools.

These forms of choice are likely to expand. The new federal No Child Left Behind Act requires school districts to provide choices, including charters and other alternatives to children attending schools defined as consistently failing to meet performance targets.[2] By states' own standards, more than 4,800 schools out of some 93,000 did not meet their performance targets during the 2002-2003 school year.

Among the ways in which options are increasing in education:

- Estimates indicate that some 610,000 students are enrolled in "alternative schools" across the United States, schools that make a special effort to provide nurturing learning environments for young people struggling amidst the impersonality of typical large urban high schools.[3]

- Similarly, "magnet" schools (specialist schools concentrating on foreign language, math and science, or the arts) are now common in public education. According to the Education Commission of the States, 33 states reported in 1999-2000 that they contained more than 1,350 magnet schools.[4]

- Most urban districts have at some point contracted for extremely expensive residential treatment (in the private, sometimes for-profit, world) for students with severe disabilities.[5]

- Some large school districts offer parents relatively unconstrained choices among public schools within the district. These programs frequently require that oversubscribed schools choose among students based on priorities emphasizing such variables as geographic proximity, enrollment with siblings, and race and ethnic balance.[6]

- Publicly funded voucher programs, intended to expand choices for low-income families in inner-city neighborhoods, exist in Milwaukee and Cleveland. These encourage parents to enroll their children in private schools (some of them religious). The U.S. Supreme Court decision found such vouchers constitutionally acceptable in Cleveland, and it refused to review a lower court decision approving the Milwaukee program.[7]

- State-funded voucher programs exist in six states— Colorado, Wisconsin, Ohio, Florida, Vermont, and Maine. Three states—Arizona, Florida, and Pennsylvania—also allow income tax deductions for contributions to private voucher programs.

- Forty-one states have enacted legislation providing for charter schools, and some 2,700 charter schools, enrolling more than 500,000 children, now exist in the United States.[8]

- Privately financed voucher programs for low-income children exist in more than 100 cities in the United States.

- In 1999, some 850,000 children were being schooled at home, according to the National Center on Education Statistics.[9]

Today's public education system encompasses a large and growing number of options providing significant choice to American parents with regard to their children's education. As a consequence, the discussion about "choice" is not about "whether," but rather is about "what kind" and "how much?" It is no longer accurate to think of public education as incompatible with (or antithetical to) choice. Community leaders, public officials, and citizens need to consider how the expansion of choice can be structured so that publicly funded schools of all kinds work effectively for all of America's children.

The Choice Debate

At its worst, the public debate about choice is partisan, shedding more heat than light on the subject. Pitting ideologues on both sides of the question against each other, it is reminiscent of political campaigns at their worst, complete with personal attacks and attributions of base motives. The debate over choice is too rarely what it should be: a reasoned discussion of alternative arrangements for educating children.

Extreme Views

The most extreme pro-choice position is that public schools left to themselves will never improve and that

Choosing in Seattle

The Seattle School District, with an enrollment of 48,000, is thought to provide one of the most comprehensive open choice plans in the country. Although the district encourages parents to choose any public school in the city for their children, parents are not guaranteed the school of their choice.

The details vary somewhat for elementary, middle, and secondary schools, but here are the basic rules:

- Elementary and middle school students are assigned to a "reference area" (based on home address) within which students receive enrollment priority for their area school.

- Groups of elementary and middle schools are divided into "clusters" or "regions" (with at least one alternative school per cluster) for which area students enjoy priority. District transportation is provided. Transportation is not provided outside a cluster.

- When there are more applicants than spaces at a particular school, "tie-breakers" involving siblings, reference area, distance to school, and lotteries are used. Integration was also a tie-breaker until upper-income parents challenged it in court.

- "Enrollment centers" throughout the district provide basic information about schools and answer questions about enrollment procedures.

- Early registration helps and parents have the right to appeal school assignment.

Source: Great Schools Net: http://www.greatschools.net

market forces alone are enough to produce both quality and fairness in education. Ideologues on the right claim that public schools have become little more than coalitions of intransigent unions protecting incompetent teachers, recalcitrant bureaucrats defending the status quo, and politically motivated school board members worrying about the next election. To extreme choice supporters, anyone opposing choice is doing so to protect their own political or economic advantage.

The most strident case against choice is that market forces inevitably corrupt public purposes. This view holds that public school districts alone can be trusted to work in the public interest. Opponents say that markets are incompatible with the goals of public education, both because they always produce winners and losers and because they systematically put the interests of individuals above the public interest in education. Ideologues on the left claim that choice and competition will stratify schools by race, class, and religion, while making them less accountable to the public.

More Nuanced Views

At the extremes in the public discussion, not a lot of common ground exists between advocates and opponents of more options in education. But more nuanced cases can be (and are) made by thoughtful analysts on both sides. These positions take seriously both the reasonable hopes of choice proponents and the reasonable concerns of skeptics.

Choice supporters argue that a monopolistic enterprise in education can be no more effective in the public sector than it proved to be in the private sector.[10] In this view, expanding choice is a way to cut through an accretion of decades of regulations, contracts, and court orders that tie many systems, particularly large urban ones, in knots. Choice becomes not an attack on public schools, but a new way of providing public education. Choice supporters are convinced that by putting schools in a situation where they must demonstrate performance or lose out to competitors, choice both creates incentives for improvement and encourages the spread of good new ideas.

In particular, they argue, the only students who do not enjoy choice now are the poor. Opening up new options may be a way to release poor children from schools that have failed them and their communities for years. In this line of thinking, a lot of attention is paid to the fact that middle-income families can "choose" for their children by moving into nice neighborhoods and by using personal influence to get the best teachers and instructional programs. Well-to-do families can "choose" among public schools by moving to different communities. They can also pursue private choices by paying tuition.

In the end, choice proponents rest their case on a belief that a system that creates options and responds to parent demands will introduce valuable elements of the market that will make most children's schools better and few children's schools worse. Although at the outset many poor families may lack experience with choosing schools, they will quickly learn how to distinguish between schools that serve their children well and those that do not. The hope is that competition among schools will lead to innovation of successful approaches to schooling and imitation of successful schools.

Choice opponents also make a more nuanced argument. They argue that state policies everywhere require students to attend school and public officials cannot be indifferent to the outcomes of the education provided at public expense. Many choice opponents agree that fewer strings should be attached to federal and state funds, with much greater freedom of action offered at the district and school level. Willing to concede that more options might permit some students to get a better education than they now receive, opponents nevertheless worry that the process of improvement promised by choice advocates will be too weak to lead to a general upgrading of all schools. They fear that as the ablest students and teachers leave for newly available schools and options, the students and the schools that remain behind will be worse off.

Conceding that the poor are often at a disadvantage in the current climate, some choice opponents argue that the solution lies in equalizing funding and upgrading existing schools so that all students have equal opportunities to learn. They are convinced that the private sector doesn't have any special knowledge about how to provide good public services.

Critics don't think the existence of private choices for middle- or upper-income groups justifies expanding choice to all families. In a mixed economy, those with resources can buy their way out of any number of things (including public transportation and the postal service, for example), but that does not constitute an argument for ending direct government provision of those services. Above all, choice opponents worry that families now suffering from lack of choice will suffer even more in a more competitive environment. In this view, inexperienced choosers run the risk of serving as easy prey for fly-by-night school providers, just as they have from shoddy proprietary programs in postsecondary education.

What Is Choice?

Making sense of the debate about choice is made immeasurably more difficult by the lack of definition of key terms. In particular, choice advocates and opponents frequently talk past each other by failing to define what they mean. As noted above, there is already a considerable amount of "choice" in some school districts, and many districts already let some families choose among privately provided options. Since public agencies are already providing many choices, the dispute must be about more than whether it is good for families to choose.

The Commission offers a simple definition of school choice, which can apply to many different situations. Choice is any arrangement that allows parents to decide which of two or more publicly funded schools their child will attend.

The Commission identified an eight-stage continuum of choice policies. The stages become more complex and publicly controversial as the supply side of the school choice issue becomes more independent of the district. The eight stages are as follows:

1. All students are assigned to schools by the district—no choice.

2. District allows some families to choose among district-run alternative or magnet schools.

3. District allows all families to choose among all district-run schools.

4. District also allows families to choose some district-authorized schools operated by independent parties (charters).

5. Families may choose among district-run and chartered schools and also schools chartered by other government entities.

6. Families may choose among many publicly funded schools, all of which are operated by independent parties (charter districts).

7. Families receive vouchers but must use them only in approved schools that must employ admissions lotteries and accept vouchers as full payment of tuition.

8. Families receive vouchers that they may use in any school, while schools set their own admissions and tuition policies.

This continuum goes from no choice of any kind to choice that is totally unregulated. In between it includes six kinds of choice that are essentially public, in that government defines at least some elements of who chooses, what may be chosen, how schools are funded, and how they may operate. In the first seven stages, in short, there exists at least the possibility of public oversight of significant dimensions of schooling.[11] Only the last stage (unregulated vouchers) has not been adopted as a matter of public policy in at least a few jurisdictions.

What this continuum raises is the question of what it means to be a public school. The current definition assumes that a "public school" is one that is financed, staffed, owned, and overseen by a government agency. The continuum above opens up the possibility of a new

Vouchers in Cleveland

In June 2002, the U.S. Supreme Court held that Cleveland's state-enacted school voucher program does not violate the U.S. Constitution. In *Zelman v. Simmons-Harris*, the Court ruled that the Cleveland program "is entirely neutral with respect to religion," because it is "a program of true private choice." In a concurring opinion, Justice Sandra Day O'Connor wrote, "The support that the Cleveland voucher program provides religious institutions is neither substantial nor atypical of existing government programs."

The Cleveland program, enacted by the Ohio legislature in 1995, originally paid up to $2,250 in tuition for each student to attend private schools in the city or public schools in the suburbs. In recent years, more than 4,000 students have participated in the program in 49 participating city private schools. Scholarships to private schools were capped at $2,250 or the amount of tuition, whichever was less, with private schools prohibited from charging more than $2,500. Suburban public schools accepting vouchers received the voucher plus the normal amount of per-pupil state aid, for a total of about $6,500 annually per student. No suburban public schools participated in the program.

Vouchers in Cleveland have not been a financial boon to private schools. Catholic educators and others argue it has been a net drain on the resources of voucher schools and the parishes that run them. At least three Catholic parochial schools, some with 60% or more of their enrollment made up of voucher students, closed their doors at the end of the 2001-2002 school year citing declining enrollments or financial difficulties.

Source: Mary Ann Zehr, "Cleveland Voucher Aid No Panacea for Hard-Pressed Catholic Schools." *Education Week,* June 18, 2003.

definition, namely a school that is financed with public funds and overseen by government agencies, but staffed and operated by independent organizations.

Religious issues complicate the challenge of choice. For almost half a century, church-state controversies have created a steady stream of school litigation. Until recently, the idea of public assistance to help students in private schools (or religious schools) seemed politically and legally impractical. For several decades, the weight of judicial opinion focused on interpreting First Amendment prohibitions against establishing religion (the Establishment Clause). Recently, however, the Free Exercise of Religion Clause has seemed to prevail. In 2002, the Supreme Court in a 5-4 ruling extended this thinking in *Zelman v. Simmons-Harris.*[12] The Court ruled the participation of religious schools in a state-funded voucher program in Cleveland was acceptable on the grounds that parents, not the government, made the decision about the flow of funds to private schools. Even *Zelman*, it should be noted, does not endorse stage 8. The Supreme Court approved a regulated voucher program that required an admissions lottery and schools' acceptance of the voucher amount as full tuition.

Many of these forms of choice challenge a revered tradition of common schooling, which aspires to have all children in a community educated in the same schools, overseen by a local, politically accountable government agency. Although the common-school ideal is frequently violated in practice, many Americans still hold it dear and fear that choice eliminates any hope of realizing it.

Against that backdrop, and informed by available research on choice, what can we say about how community leaders, elected officials, philanthropists, and educators might structure choice? And what can be concluded about the likely consequences of different ways of proceeding?

Part 2

UNDERSTANDING HOW CHOICE MIGHT WORK

TO HELP COMMUNITY LEADERS UNDERSTAND HOW TO obtain the potential benefits of choice while avoiding its potential harms, the Commission proceeded on three fronts. First, it identified key concerns about the possible consequences of choice that most Americans consider important. Second, it reviewed the evidence available on the links between choice and those outcomes. Third, members of the Commission reasoned from what is known about how choice works to some straightforward conclusions about how choice could be designed and implemented to gain maximum benefit and avoid harm.

This part of the report defines the outcomes of greatest concern, and summarizes what the Commission learned about how choice can advance or hinder efforts to reach these objectives. Part 3 applies these lessons to the identification of issues and tradeoffs facing elected officials and community leaders as they consider choice.

Important Potential Outcomes of Choice

The Commission reviewed the current and possible effects of choice in light of the core value of public education: that all children should be thoroughly educated so that they may pursue their own dreams and contribute to a democratic, egalitarian, and prosperous American society. We examined choice in light of four potential outcomes derived from that goal:

- benefits to children whose parents exercise choice;

- benefits (or at least absence of harm) to families that do not exercise choice;

- continued pursuit of our national commitment to equal opportunity and desegregated schools; and

- advancement of common democratic values and social cohesion.

Summarizing Existing Research

There is a growing body of research on the links between choice and these outcomes. And though much of the research is rigorous and informative, it falls short of providing definitive guidance on how choice will work in every case.

Benefits to Choosers

Families choose schools (other than the school assigned) in order to gain perceived benefits, possibly including access to better instruction, more supportive school environments, or affiliation with others of similar background or values.[13] Research consistently shows that parents who choose are more satisfied with schools than parents who do not choose.[14] But studies differ on whether children whose parents choose learn more.[15] Although achievement levels in private schools and public schools of choice are often high, differences can be attributed to parents' levels of education and income, or to intangible differences between families who seek options and those who do not.[16]

The most rigorous school choice evaluations that used random assignment to control for family variables found that academic gains from vouchers were largely limited to the African-American students in their studies.[17] At least one analyst has questioned whether claims of benefits to African-American children are sufficiently supported by the data.[18] This dispute has moved into the professional statistics journals, where the latest analysis favors a positive conclusion about the effects of choice on student achievement.[19]

Research on the effectiveness of charter schools is similarly mixed. Charter schools have natural life cycles, such that schools that have been in existence for five years or more are more effective than recently opened charter schools.[20] These schools, in general, are about as effective as district-run schools serving similar students, despite the fact that charter schools generally operate with less money.[21]

Consequences for Non-Choosers

Does choice hurt children of parents who are slow to take advantage of available options? Evidence is mixed.[22] School districts that have lost children to charter schools claim that the resulting declines in their budgets are harmful because teachers leave and programs must be cut. On this basis they conclude that children in schools who lose students are put at an additional disadvantage. However, these claims have not been investigated closely.

Some states have "held harmless" their school districts, continuing to fund them as if they had not lost children to charter schools. Moreover, some school districts, especially those with growing populations and overcrowded facilities, have benefited, at least marginally, as children transferred to charter schools.

This discussion often confuses harm to schools with harm to students. Competition can cause some schools to lose students, teachers, and programs. Students who remain in such schools might or might not get poorer instruction and less attention. Schools threatened by competition might or might not find better ways to serve students.[23] Districts might or might not make special efforts to improve schools that families want to leave.[24,25] The students who go on to other schools might or might not be better off.

On average, choice programs that harm some schools might have positive, negative, or no effects

Vouchers in Milwaukee

In 1990, the Wisconsin legislature adopted a voucher program to pay for 1,000 Milwaukee students to attend secular private schools. Five years later, the legislature expanded the program to include religious schools. The law allows students who attend religious schools to opt out of religious activities and instruction with a written request from their parent or guardian. Parents of students receiving vouchers endorse checks made out to them which they sign over to the school their child will attend.

The Wisconsin statute provides for up to 15% of the Milwaukee public school students to attend private schools. To be eligible, a student's household income must be at or below designated amounts based on the household size: a two-member household may have a maximum yearly income of $21,460. Household size includes all people living in the household, and for each additional person, the maximum income is increased $5,536.

Participating private schools are allowed to use for their selection process only the information provided to them in the application. Schools are not permitted to consider the student's race, ethnic background, religion, prior test scores, grades, or membership in the church parish. Schools must accept all eligible applicants that they are able to accommodate; students are selected by a random drawing if there are more applicants than available seats.

Schools accepting voucher students are required to make "minor adjustments" for students with disabilities.

Since private schools in the state are not required to take part in standardized testing programs, it is unclear how students with vouchers in private schools (or the schools accepting vouchers) will be assessed under the requirements of the federal No Child Left Behind legislation. Participating schools must meet one of four requirements. Seventy percent of the students in the program must "advance one grade level each year"; the school's average attendance rate for students in the program must be at least 90%; at least 80% of the students in the program must "demonstrate significant academic progress;" or 70% of the families of the students in the program must meet the parent involvement criteria established by the private school.

Approximately 10,000 students attend private schools under this program at a cost of about $50 million annually.

Source: National Association of Secondary School Principals. See: www.nassp.org/services/low-down061603.cfm

Charter Schools in Michigan

Under legislation enacted in 1993, about 196 charter schools enrolling some 70,000 students exist in Michigan.

Michigan charter schools are called "public school academies." The state is one of the few offering assistance beyond per-pupil operating costs. Public school academies can borrow money for start-up at tax-exempt rates through the Michigan Municipal Bond Authority.

Michigan charters (PSAs) are state-supported public schools and they:

- may include grades K-12 or any combination of grades in between;

- are NOT permitted to charge tuition, be religiously affiliated, or screen or select students on the basis of race, religion, sex, or test scores;

- must select students for admission randomly, if the number of applicants exceeds enrollment capacity; and

- are required to follow state legislative guidelines regarding per-pupil funding, teacher certification, student transportation, and curriculum.

Source: Michigan Department of Education at: www.michigan.gov/mde/0,1607,7-140-6525_6530_6558-22947-,00.html

on students. A study of Michigan, Minnesota, and Arizona schools found that achievement increased in public schools located near charter schools.[26] Similarly, another study of charter schools in Michigan concluded that average achievement levels in public schools near charter schools increased slightly.[27] The author of the latter study concluded that scores in nearby public schools increased only because lower-achieving students went to charter schools.

Research on choice in New Zealand shows that schools that had been abandoned by most families and

teachers were allowed to continue operating.[28] Children who had been left behind were clearly left in schools with poor reputations and fewer respected teachers. New Zealand does not have a standardized testing program, so it is impossible to say for sure whether the children who stayed behind, or those who left for other schools, learned more or less.

Segregation

Does choice increase segregation?[29] The results from existing choice programs are mixed and confusing. School-level data on integration is sketchy. Voucher programs specifically targeted to low-income families have the potential to improve integration, but the extent to which this potential is realized in existing programs is unknown. Segregation is almost total in most big cities, so choice is unlikely to make it worse.[30] Even in public schools with mixed student bodies, students often segregate themselves socially.[31] That is to say, existing levels of integration, both between and within schools, are difficult to measure and hardly ideal.

There is some evidence of positive choice effects—private schools actively recruiting low-income and minority children, and greater contact between white and minority students in private schools. Some private schools appeal to people of many races, all of whom are attracted to school climate and instructional methods.[32] However, it is not known whether these private school phenomena can be reproduced in publicly supported schools of choice.

Charter schools in some states enroll a slightly more white and middle-class population than nearby public schools, but in other states charter schools serve a disproportionately low-income and minority population.[33] Much depends on the incentives embodied in state law. In states that encourage formation of charter schools to serve the most disadvantaged students, schools often serve children who are primarily from poor or minority backgrounds.[34]

Nevertheless, it is extremely difficult to say whether charter schools are more or less segregated than public schools in the surrounding district, since many districts already have schools that are overwhelmingly white or non-white.

Civic Cohesion

Americans believe that effective public education supports democracy by creating an informed citizenry capable of intelligent deliberation and willing to respect differences. Public schools are celebrated as places where children meet others from different racial, economic, and religious groups, and where habits of tolerance and accommodation are developed, in part simply by being around different people.

Choice opponents often concede that today's district-run schools are less than ideal, but they fear that choice will aggravate cultural gaps and promote separatism. Choice supporters, however, argue that ineffective or totally segregated schools cannot possibly fulfill these aspirations. Proponents claim that choice can strengthen civic life by improving basic skills instruction and by strengthening links between school and family, and between school and the broader community.

Here again the evidence is mixed. Research makes it clear that different schools have different outcomes with respect to children's civic attitudes, but it is harder to determine how schools produce these effects. Schools using the same instructional materials can produce different results in graduates. Some schools run hierarchically (e.g., traditional Catholic schools) appear to be quite powerful in helping students form pro-democratic attitudes and practices. What seems to matter as much as curriculum is the internal dynamics of the school, the implicit messages it sends about respect for individuals, the importance of open discussion, efforts to expose students to novel views of the world, and service to others as an integral part of maturing.

We do know that graduates of American private schools are more likely to vote than graduates of public schools and to express greater support for tolerance and free speech.[35] However, the most positive results come from Catholic schools, which are becoming a smaller and smaller proportion of all private schools. Students in conservative Christian schools have lower scores on tolerance than do public school students, but are as likely to participate in civic activity.[36]

There is also evidence that parents who have choices among publicly funded schools feel more effective as citizens and trust government more.[37]

In European countries where government supports schools of choice (including religious schools), scholars have frequently argued that this arrangement has, historically, supported civic cohesion.[38] In part it has done so by eliminating the need for religious groups, which would surely have struggled over control of schools, to engage in such battles. Today, however, some are questioning this traditional view, worrying that choice will operate in a different fashion as new language, ethnic, and religious groups seek public funding for their schools.

Many people in the United States express similar concerns. They fear that, given the opportunity, separatist and radical groups will operate schools openly preaching division and hatred.

Summing Up

In short, existing research paints a mixed and complicated picture. Choice could indeed lead to the benefits its supporters expect, or the harm its opponents fear. If so, the effects, both positive and negative, are less certain and more situation-dependent than advocates on either side acknowledge. One thing that is clear is that the results of choice depend on what options are made available and how they are created, supported, and designed.

Learning from Inconsistent Results

One interpretation of complex and inconsistent results is that choice itself is only indirectly linked to student learning, or for that matter to any of the other outcomes the Commission is concerned about.

All choice does is allow students to attend classes in schools other than the ones to which the public school system would have assigned them. Those classes could be better taught, more supportive, and more motivating than those in their regular public school. They could be about the same. They could be worse. Whether options lead to more learning depends on many things. Choice opens up a set of contingencies, but whether a particular child benefits depends, in part, on whether her parents manage to find and choose the right school. It depends

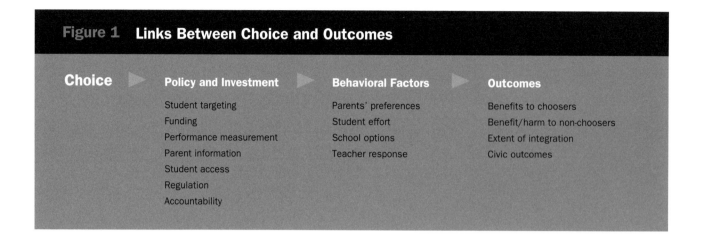

Figure 1   Links Between Choice and Outcomes

Choice ▷	Policy and Investment ▷	Behavioral Factors ▷	Outcomes
	Student targeting	Parents' preferences	Benefits to choosers
	Funding	Student effort	Benefit/harm to non-choosers
	Performance measurement	School options	Extent of integration
	Parent information	Teacher response	Civic outcomes
	Student access		
	Regulation		
	Accountability		

on whether the school provides the learning experiences it promises. And it depends on a host of other issues as well, including the child's health and how assiduously the child works.

Similar considerations apply with respect to integration, effects on children whose parents are slow to take advantage of choice, and civic cohesion.[39] The effects depend not on choice itself, but on how it is designed, the specific conditions under which it is introduced, and what actions educators, families, and government subsequently take.

The effort to generalize about new options and choice—to say what its effects are on average—is important. Still, it does not tell parents, educators, or policymakers what they most need to know. That is to say it does not tell any of these groups whether their particular local situation is an appropriate one for expanding choice, much less about how to structure choice to promote its best outcomes and avoid its worst. If choice is to be more widely adopted, a change in how people think about it is required. The national conversation is, too frequently, grounded in a simplistic model of stimulus and response— that is, that choice leads inevitably to some outcome or other, whether good or bad. A more realistic model for the national conversation would be that choice leads to outcomes only indirectly. This more sophisticated view holds that the effects of choice depend at least in part on other factors, such as rules, investments, individual behavior, and the economic and social context in which it operates.

Understanding How Choice Works

The Commission tried to open up the "black box" of choice, the complex framework linking choice policy to important results. We hoped to go beyond measuring the correlation between choice and key outcomes—for instance, how well the children of parents who choose learn—to understand how such results come about. Thus, for example, in examining the process by which choice might lead to greater student learning, the Commission identified many intervening factors, such as parents' information about choices, the existence of options, and a match between options and a child's needs and interests. The Commission made similar sketches of the links between choice and other outcomes, including consequences for non-choosers, segregation, and civic cohesion.

Figure 1 identifies the key factors that appeared in almost every sketch of the links between choice and important outcomes. Most of these factors are policies and investments that communities can make in the course of designing choice programs. Figure 1 also identifies four linking factors—parents' preferences, student effort, school options, and teacher response—that stand between policies and investments and the outcomes of choice. The linking factors depend on the behavior of individuals—parents, teachers, and school providers— in response to policies and investments. The remainder of this section will define the links in Figure 1 and show why each is important.

Student Targeting

Poor and disadvantaged students generally have less access to schooling options. Choice opponents rightly worry that more-advantaged families may seize most attractive new options. Targeting choice, by specifying that poor and disadvantaged students are to be first in line for new options, is an obvious antidote. Targeting requires administration and invites controversy. Families immediately above the "cut-off" point, wherever it is set, will inevitably campaign to change the criteria. However, if the motive for a state or local choice initiative is to serve poor children or children now trapped in bad schools, some form of targeting is necessary.

Funding

The amount and stability of money following children to the schools they attend is clearly important. Although there is some dispute about how much money states are obligated to spend on children's education, there is some minimum level of funding below which few schools could operate. Scant funding limits how many school options can arise, the kind of instruction they can provide, and how long they can survive. Funding also affects schools' ability to serve disadvantaged and handicapped students. Low-income, handicapped, and non-English speaking students typically cost more to educate, and unless funding reflects this reality, schools would have an incentive to avoid such students.

Performance Measurement

School performance measures are important for two reasons. First, parents choosing schools need a basis of comparison.[40] Measurements of how much children learn in a school—changes in test scores from one year to the next for an individual—can factor out differences in students' incoming test scores and help parents identify the school in which their child is most likely to thrive. Second, school performance information allows government to exercise its responsibility to ensure that all children get an adequate education. Testing is controversial but most people agree that testing in core subjects—in literacy and mathematics for elementary schools, and in understanding

vocabulary, text, and themes, and basic algebra for secondary schools—is a reasonable minimum. If choice is to lead to real options among schools, there must be some common testing, just enough to give parents and the state good information about schools' basic performance on core skills. Individual schools might opt for additional testing for self-assessment or to back up claims of high performance in particular areas.

Parent Information

When districts assign students to schools, parents do not need much information. But if parents are to choose, they need a lot.[41] Choice in the absence of information can only lead to poorly informed decisions. Parents need to know not simply that they have options and that their children are eligible, but what the options are, how they differ, and how to distinguish programs that will benefit their children from those that will not serve them well. Better information, however, does not guarantee that parents will select the best school or avoid the trap of confounding test results with socio-economic background.

Student Access

Choice means little if there are no school options available, or if some groups of students are shut out of desirable schools. Access implies first that admissions processes will be fair and open, and that groups of students will not be denied choice simply because their families cannot arrange transportation.

Regulation

Choice is one way a state can meet its obligation to ensure that children get a good education. States can trust parents and independent school providers to some extent, but they must take reasonable steps to ensure that students learn what they need to make a living and participate in civic life. This implies the need for some clarity about the minima all children must learn before high school graduation and possibly benchmarks for anticipated skills development at certain grade levels. Performance measurement and parent information can provide some regulatory structure. States also have the authority to mandate curriculum, but in areas where links between practice and outcomes are unproven, mandates can squelch experimentation and competition.

Accountability

What happens if a school performs well or badly? Who acts? And what are the consequences?[42] Choice implies that parents can reward and punish schools by enrolling or withdrawing—or threatening to withdraw—their children. However, choice does not rule out schools answering to government as well as parents.[43] Existing state and federal policies, including state standards-based reform laws and the federal No Child Left Behind Act, impose certain testing requirements and threaten penalties to low-performing schools. These requirements are incompatible with forms of choice that make schools accountable only to parents, but they can work with schemes in which schools are accountable to both parents and government. Government can specify academic outcomes that schools should attain and withdraw financial support from failing schools. Like parents, it can also take intermediate steps with low-performing schools—publicizing failures, threatening to cancel licenses or charters, and even opening other schools nearby to compete for students.

Behavioral Factors

Parents' Preferences

For the children of choosers to benefit from choice, parents must have some desire to put their children into schools that teach effectively. Parents who are indifferent about school effectiveness or who put other factors, such as school location or clubs and sports, above academics, will get a more effective school only by accident. Parent preferences also help determine whether choice leads to greater school segregation and better or worse civic outcomes. No one knows for sure what parents would choose if they had many choices and some experience with selecting schools and living with the consequences. Private school parents apparently prefer

racially mixed student bodies under some circumstances,[44] and so might public school parents if they knew some schools offered both integration and quality instruction. When choice is first introduced, parent preferences are likely to be less clear and predictable than they might be after parents have had time to make choices and observe the consequences.[45]

Student Effort

No matter how hard and efficiently adults work, learning depends to a great extent on student effort. One case for choice is that it can create mutual leverage and expectations between families and schools, and that these in turn motivate students to work hard.[46] This hope, if it is to be met, requires that parents find schools in which they can be confident, and that teachers and administrators take parents seriously. It also assumes that children whose parents choose will find their new school a good fit, instructionally, motivationally, and socially. Choice can, if options available in a locality are stable and well-understood, allow schools to develop long-term relationships with families, stable staffs, and coherent instructional programs.[47]

School Options

Every outcome of choice depends at least in part on what kinds of schools become available.[48] The hope that choice will lead to greater student learning assumes either that new options will arise or that competition will lead existing schools to improve. Even the fear that choice can harm civic cohesion is based partly on the assumption that new schools will be run and staffed by people who care less about tolerance, diversity, and community than do the leaders and teachers in district-run schools. The school supply response to choice—what schools arise and what they teach and for what reasons—depends heavily on rules and funding.[49] Low funding of alternatives discourages schools from serving challenging student populations. It also favors schools with other sources of support (for example, schools with philanthropic support or parochial schools that receive support from their parishes).

Teacher Response

Many hopes and fears about choice are based on assumptions about the behavior of teachers. Most forms of choice leave teacher hiring and firing to individual schools and weaken controls on teacher placement derived from collective bargaining agreements. Choice can lead to general improvement in school performance if more capable people seek teaching jobs and if competition leads current teachers to upgrade their own training and performance.[50] However, choice might lead to general decline in school performance if fewer people want to teach or the most capable current teachers either cluster in the most privileged schools or leave the profession.

What "It Depends…" Implies for Policy

All of the outcomes that concern us—whether children of choosers benefit, whether students whose parents are slow to choose are unharmed, and whether segregation and social stratification increase or not—depend on combinations of these eleven linking factors.

Because so much depends on how these factors are combined and interrelate, choice is unlikely to be the panacea for American schools trumpeted by its advocates. And it is equally unlikely to be the death of public support for American education, the fear of its detractors. There is nothing automatic about choice. The links between choice and its outcomes are not so mechanical that outcomes can be totally controlled or perfectly predicted. Choice's outcomes, good or bad, depend heavily on how communities structure and implement it.

Whatever consequences choice has, for results both desirable and undesirable, they are contingent. The results of choice depend on how it is defined, established, and organized. That is to say, the investments and policies that governments make to introduce and support new options are what will enable educators, private organizations, and parents to perform their essential tasks.

The Arizona Charter Experience

With the most pro-choice policies in the nation, Arizona has some 375 charter school sites, enrolling about 65,000 students, and has been hailed as a "free market in public education."

Charter operators determine curriculum, hire and fire teachers, and earn funding based on the number of parents who choose their school. Unlike private schools, Arizona charter schools cannot require religious instruction for their students, charge tuition, or deny students admission.

A major evaluation of Arizona's experiment in charters finds that while choice has not been a panacea, it has made schools more accountable to parents and has empowered many teachers.

After three years of exponential expansion, charter enrollment growth has slowed somewhat since 1998. Nearly 95% of Arizona public school students remain in district schools; charter enrollment is expected to stabilize at 7% to 15% of district enrollments.

It seems that charter schools don't replace district schools, but they push district schools to compete. In Arizona, state subsidies follow students, so charter enrollments are watched closely by district school administrators who fear loss of students.

Some district schools react to competition by advertising, opening magnet schools, and changing the curriculum. Competition pushes many district schools to work to win back charter parents.

The Arizona Department of Education posts report cards for all public schools on the Internet to help parents select schools. The report cards list school test scores, curriculum, mission statements, and other data.

Source: Center for Education Reform: edreform.com

Part 3

IMPLICATIONS

WHAT DOES THE EVIDENCE PRESENTED EARLIER IMPLY FOR elected officials and community leaders? Can it help them think about whether choice holds any promise for improving public education in their communities? Can it be used to explore how to design and implement choice so as to obtain needed benefits without doing harm? This section explores these questions. Although this chapter draws on the evidence presented earlier, it also draws reasonable inferences from that evidence in an effort to provide policy guidance.

In education policy, just as in business, there is no free lunch. In the design of choice programs it is possible to preserve some values, like close government supervision of schools, only by trading off others, such as creation of new options. Similarly, it is possible to squeeze the amounts of public funds that move with children as their parents choose alternative schools, but only at the expense of more ambitious options and innovation.

Figure 2 displays the "no free lunch" message graphically (see page 30). It illustrates how the intersection of two different areas of policy—prescription versus flexibility and generous funding of options versus limited funding—creates four separate quadrants. Each of the four represents a different reality. "Low prescription" refers to policies that impose few requirements on schools. A low prescription approach implies little or no performance measurement, light demands for parent information, few constraints on how schools admit students, little regulation of what is taught and who may teach, no restrictions on whether "choice" schools can supplement their public per-pupil fees, and accountability that relies largely on parental choice. "High prescription" refers to the opposite. Here, policy provides explicit requirements, including clear statements about consumer information, rules about performance measurement, lotteries for student admission, and explicit expectations about curriculum, mixing of public

and private funds, and teacher hiring, plus public involvement in accountability.

What is clear immediately from Figure 2 is that communities that regulate new schools tightly are likely to get few options, even if they provide relatively generous funding. Unfortunately, whether in quadrants A or C, high levels of prescription do not encourage much choice or the development of many new options. The major benefit is that these districts risk little; the major disadvantage is that they do not gain very much.

Communities that create a situation putting them in quadrant D on the other hand (limited funding and low prescription) gain little while running a lot of risks. Providing relatively small amounts of money with little oversight is unlikely to create ambitious new options or generate much teacher response. The major danger in quadrant D is that new options will be developed by naïve or zealous groups willing to accept responsibility for starting a school without receiving enough funds to do the job.

Quadrant B is the place to be if communities genuinely want to provide new options, encourage teacher response, and ensure benefits to choosers. But quadrant B contains some risks. Communities that provide full funding for new options along with low prescription may have to worry about damage to existing schools, increased segregation or social stratification, and other negative outcomes. Communities that want to avoid such negative outcomes could move slightly in the direction of greater prescription—for example, by adopting arrangements like chartering that allow public agencies to screen potential school providers in advance and hold schools accountable for performance.[51]

While Figure 2 makes crude distinctions, it can be used to classify existing choice programs. In truth, quadrant A—generous funding and high prescription—looks very much like the provisions governing charter schools in New York State. Quadrant B—generous funding and low prescription—resembles the Milwaukee voucher program. The Michigan charter program seems to fit into

quadrant C—low funding and high prescription, while quadrant D—low funding and low to moderate prescription—can describe both Arizona charter schools and the Cleveland voucher program.

Implications of Generous Versus Low Funding

State and local leaders considering expansion of choice face important decisions about funding.[52] If the effort to expand children's options provides schools with relatively little operating money (substantially less than the average district per-pupil expenditure), the supply response will

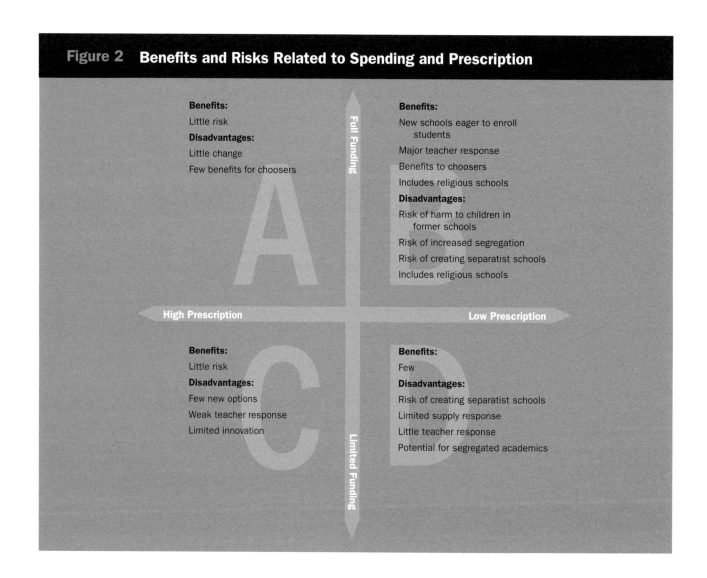

Figure 2   Benefits and Risks Related to Spending and Prescription

Full Funding

Benefits:
Little risk
Disadvantages:
Little change
Few benefits for choosers

Benefits:
New schools eager to enroll
    students
Major teacher response
Benefits to choosers
Includes religious schools
Disadvantages:
Risk of harm to children in
    former schools
Risk of increased segregation
Risk of creating separatist schools
Includes religious schools

High Prescription   Low Prescription

Benefits:
Little risk
Disadvantages:
Few new options
Weak teacher response
Limited innovation

Benefits:
Few
Disadvantages:
Risk of creating separatist schools
Limited supply response
Little teacher response
Potential for segregated academics

Limited Funding

be weak. A similar point must be made about capital costs. If schools offering new options must pay directly for facilities while existing district-run schools benefit from separate accounts for capital expenditures, new options will be reduced. In general, states and localities need to consider whether there is any warrant for spending less on a student just because his or her parents have chosen a school that is not run by a school district.

However, state and local leaders face pressures to spend less on new options than on existing schools. School districts point to fixed costs to manage a central office and operate school buildings, including those losing students to competitors. They also point out that the marginal cost of educating one extra pupil is less than the per-pupil average cost. If a student leaving a district-run school takes with him the average rather than the marginal cost of education, the school left behind suffers a noticeable financial loss.

In the past, many state legislatures have resolved this conflict by tilting toward existing district schools. Most have offered new charter schools less than the total available from combined state and local per-pupil expenditures. In addition, they have required charters to rent their own facilities and arrange their own transportation. Some have continued to fund district-run schools as if their enrollment were unaffected by students' departure for charter schools.

Such decisions have consequences. Paying schools that offer new options much less than is available to run existing schools limits what new schools can offer. It makes it less likely that new-options schools will seek to educate challenging students, while increasing the likelihood of segregation. In some sense, it also penalizes students whose parents choose new options, implying that a parent's choice somehow reduces the community's responsibility. Maintaining district schools' funding, even as students leave, also insulates those schools from the effects of competition and reduces their incentive to improve.

Without careful thought in advance about design, choice programs can have unintended consequences. In Cleveland, for example, the dollar value of the voucher was so small relative to the per-pupil funding for state charter schools (now $2,700 versus $6,100) that many schools converted to charter status and stopped accepting vouchers. This reduced the supply of schools available to voucher students, frustrating an important goal of the Cleveland voucher program.

Policy entrepreneurs working to enact choice programs understandably prefer to make the transformation appear to be straightforward and inexpensive.[53] The result, however, is that many choice proposals are not constructed to get the desired results. For example, California ballot initiatives in 1993 and 2000 would have provided vouchers worth far less than the cost of educating children in public schools ($2,600 in 1993 and $4,000 in 2000). In addition, they did not target the poor. The first Bush Administration proposed a $1,500 federally funded voucher for poor children. These programs might have benefited families able to gain access to inexpensive parochial schools (and to pay some additional tuition) but most low-income families could not have used them. Lax public oversight of Arizona's 65,000-student charter school program has led to scandals and demands for new regulations that may force closure of many schools. Few students (only 3%) participated in Minnesota's statewide choice program, in part, apparently, because out-of-area transportation was not available. In general, decisions about how to fund expansions of choice, like most significant public policy actions, involve important tradeoffs among legitimate interests. But it also seems to be generally true that good education, in either a choice or a non-choice environment, is not possible on the cheap.

Implications of High Versus Low Prescription

The amount and level of regulation is also a major policy variable. If schools that expand options for children face the same rules and constraints as existing district-run schools (high prescription in Figure 2) the supply response will be limited. However, if new-options schools face few rules and constraints, communities run some significant risks. Disadvantaged students might not gain access to new options. Schools might ignore the teaching of basic skills, shortchange democratic values, or become more stratified by race or income. Poorly managed new schools could conceivably go under, leaving students, parents, teachers, and the community in crisis. These risks are serious in some communities and trivial in others.

Nobody favors over-regulation of the sort that mires schools in bureaucratic make-work interfering with teaching and learning. The challenge, in part, becomes how to encourage a system of schools offering high-quality teaching, learning, curriculum, and assessment without impeding useful and desirable innovation and local initiative. As Figure 2 illustrates, the more localities constrain choice with prescription, the fewer options they are likely to obtain. Conversely, the more they restrain prescription, the more choice they will encourage.

More choice, however, is accompanied by more questions. For example, as Figure 2 notes, communities in quadrant B will face the issue of whether to finance the education of students attending religious schools. Funding students in schools espousing a particular faith raises other challenges. Can faith-based schools compel religious study for non-believers? Should they be required to accept non-believers? If religious schools hire or teach "for mission," would that permit the teaching of creationism, discriminating on the basis of race, gender, or sexual orientation, or hiring only members of the faith? These are complex legal and philosophical issues that cannot be fully resolved by research. But many of them will require attention at the local level as communities consider the design of choice.

Designing Options to Achieve Particular Results

It is not written anywhere that policymakers or community leaders have to put choice in place while hoping for the best. Policymakers can make conscious decisions to design new choice options in the hopes of getting particular results. How can communities proceed if they want choice to produce positive results—increased learning for students of families who choose, and benefits to children whose families

are slow to exercise choice—and avoid negative outcomes, such as segregation or harm to social cohesion?

Learning For Children Whose Families Choose

If children whose families choose are to benefit, the families must have quality options and be able to choose based on good information. Accordingly, providers of new schools need the resources and freedom of action necessary to provide good instruction. To do this, providers need both to hire teachers on the basis of "fit" with the school's approach to instruction, and to attract students and parents on the basis of their distinctive offerings. Options are likely to be higher quality if new schools receive per-pupil funding at least roughly comparable to that of district-managed schools.

Addressing the needs of the disadvantaged (or those now in low-performing schools) requires making sure that choice is targeted to poor or disadvantaged students, that per-pupil funding is weighted in favor of students with disabilities or other special learning needs, and that participating schools accept public funding as payment in full, without requiring families to pay more. These provisions reduce schools' incentive to handpick students who are easiest to educate or whose families have the greatest resources.

Transportation is already provided to students attending most public schools located any distance from their homes. If families must arrange their own transportation to distant schools of choice, children in poor families might not get full access to the available opportunities.

Even in total, these actions do not guarantee that disadvantaged students will benefit from expansion of choice. Still, they provide the conditions under which that desirable outcome is possible.

Avoiding Harm to Children of Parents Who Are Slow to Choose

A different challenge is presented in trying to make sure that children remaining in district-run schools benefit from choice. Communities that want to protect children who remain in district schools would make sure that schools threatened by competition get at least the same real, per-dollar funding as other district-run schools, and are free to hire teachers, set pay for staff with rare or critical skills, and make tradeoffs between salaries and purchase of new methods and materials.[54] They would also buffer such schools from very rapid or unpredictable changes in revenue or staffing. Teachers in these schools would also receive the full benefit of public investments in teacher training and other school-performance upgrades.

Avoiding Segregation

Segregation, one of the most difficult educational challenges facing the United States, will also require attention in a choice environment. Communities that want to make sure choice does not lead to greater segregation would want to take all the actions listed above. In addition, these communities would sponsor information campaigns to ensure that both poor and minority parents understand the options available to them and conduct or oversee scrupulously fair admissions processes for all schools, including lotteries for those oversubscribed. Communities determined to avoid segregation would also require participating schools to accept public funding as full tuition, so that poor families do not need to "add on" with their own funds. These communities would also withdraw public funding from schools that target poor or minority students for discipline or expulsion.

Policy on segregation is complicated by the fact that some schools intend—for good reasons based in the public interest—to provide specialized instruction and appeal to children with special needs and aptitudes. Many big public school systems offer arts and science magnets, schools for students who want to prepare for specific careers, and schools providing special help to immigrants. Some even offer Afro-centric, language-immersion, and single-sex schools. Increasing choice implies that even more such schools might become available. As is the case with district-run schools, individual schools under choice might attract a clientele that is poorer, whiter, blacker, or more female than the district average. Communities need to distinguish between these effects of specialization and the effects of conscious efforts to exclude minority students.

Avoiding Harm to Social Cohesion

Another knotty problem of public policy demands attention in a choice environment. Communities that want to ensure that choice does not lead to the establishment of schools that stratify students by income, class, or race or teach hatred or discrimination need to do everything listed above. But they also need to bear in mind that the links between modes of schooling and civic outcomes are not well-understood, and many prescriptions that might look obvious to some will look arbitrary to others. Communities concerned about civic cohesion might:

• require teaching of core civics courses emphasizing the values of equality, democracy, tolerance, and Constitutional principles of equality and freedom of speech;

• create incentives for effective civics-oriented teaching by measuring student attitudes and reporting results on school exit exams; and

• establish clear policies on investigation of complaints about schools that may have violated their commitments to avoid separatist teaching and cancellation of licenses for schools found to have done so.

These simple "If… then…" statements do not say exactly how a particular community should structure choice. Though some will consider the observations above to be obvious, in fact few if any choice programs in the United States have been designed with these contingencies in mind. In general, programs structured to meet particular goals are much more likely to succeed than those that ignore the linkages explored in Part 2 of this document.

The Costs of Prescription to Protect the Advantaged

In addition to prescriptions to target benefits to the disadvantaged and exercise some quality control over new options, state and local leaders will come under pressure to protect some groups. Choice implies transparency of resource allocation—funds follow children—

and new schools' freedom to choose teachers on the basis of fit. Some public policies are now built on quite different premises.

Current district policies, expressed in teacher collective bargaining agreements, allow the most experienced (and expensive) teachers to avoid low-income and minority schools by transferring to schools in better neighborhoods. District policies that let schools in attractive neighborhoods fill their slots with highly paid experienced teachers and insulate those schools from high salary costs by charging them only district-wide average teacher salaries encourage experienced teachers to avoid challenging schools. Schools serving middle-class students, and senior teachers, benefit disproportionately from these existing policies.[55]

The consequence of these policies is that schools serving poor and minority students generally get the newest and least experienced teachers.[56] Because teacher salary funds are tied up in more-advantaged schools (where higher-paid teachers work), schools in poor neighborhoods get no compensating advantages—neither more uncommitted funds to spend nor more teachers to reduce class size.

Expanding choice in ways that avoid harm to the poorest children requires changes in the ways school districts allocate funds internally. Effective choice requires a pattern of transparency in resource allocation. Districts must make sure they truly spend as much money on poor pupils as on middle-class ones. Since this will mean that many schools serving disadvantaged students get more money than they do currently, these schools must be free to offer higher salaries, hire more teachers, or invest in new training and technology that might increase teacher productivity.

Forms of prescription that protect those with the greatest advantages conflict with efforts to help the disadvantaged. It is possible to expand choice a little bit without changing the ways districts do their business. But some important objectives—especially avoiding harm to students in public schools that come under competitive pressure—require school district change as well.

Phasing in Choice

In communities that consider choice a way to open new possibilities for disadvantaged children, a planned transition, with investments in new capacities, will be needed. There is no way a community can establish all the "right" policies and make all the "right" decisions and investments in advance. While policymakers and analysts already understand a great deal about choice, the most important lessons can be learned only by doing. Saying "we can't try choice until all the questions are answered" is equivalent to saying "we will never try it."

State and community leaders, elected officials, and philanthropists can make significant contributions to efforts to improve design and implementation of choice. Figure 3 lays out their most important roles.

Elected officials can decide whether to ensure that parents understand their choices or leave it to chance. Similarly, they can run fair lotteries or let schools handpick their students. They can either create a stable regulatory environment to encourage development of school options or discourage development of new options by giving new schools too little money while subjecting them to fickle oversight. Public officials can also decide whether to make sensible investments in parent information, common performance standards, and outreach to poor parents, or they can make do with whatever the current public agencies have put in place.

Challenges are greatest to government. It has to build several capacities that state governments and school districts now lack. In addition to allocating funds on a per-pupil basis, providing good information, and running fair admissions lotteries, government must do things it has always had difficulty doing in education. It needs to create an environment of fair competition and reliable rules so that both alternative and district-run schools have a chance to offer effective instruction. It also needs to: 1) establish common student-performance standards that can be defended as bases for determining whether schools are eligible to receive public funds, and 2) take the school licensing and de-licensing process seriously as an administrative function based on school performance, not political pressure.

Figure 3   Roles of Key Actors

	Policies	Investments
Local	Create transparent student-based budgets Amend collective bargaining agreements to allow school-level hiring Create admissions oversight agency Allow schools to buy services from central office or private vendors	Fund parent information and outreach programs Create capacity to analyze and report on performance of all publicly funded schools Create capacity for auditing individual school spending Create ombudsman to look into discrimination claims
State	Re-mission local agencies to charter and license schools of choice Consolidate funding streams Fund schools on a per-student basis Amend collective bargaining laws to allow individual schools to hire teachers	Rebuild standards and tests to provide basic performance information on a value added basis Fund statewide dissemination of lessons learned from choice initiatives
Federal	Consolidate funding streams Allow Title I eligibility to become a weight in per-pupil funding schemes	Fund research on interactions between student and school characteristics in determining learning outcomes Fund choice information centers for state and community leaders
Foundations	Sponsor community-wide planning for choice Sponsor analysis of policy options Create reform watchdog groups to oversee implementation of choice programs and suggest correctives	Provide venture capital for new schools Support research on how parents use information and how parents can learn to judge schools Fund local parent information fairs and outreach Help new schools find low-cost facilities Support studies of district-run schools that have improved even as they lost students to other alternatives

Note that these daunting requirements are not all new: State standards-based reform laws and the federal No Child left Behind Act all assume that government will fund schools equitably, oversee them on the basis of performance, and create options for children whose schools do not help them achieve.

There will always be a need for state and local oversight agencies, but existing school districts, designed for centralized control of funds and teacher assignment, might not be up to the task of overseeing choice. States probably need either to re-mission school districts or create new entities whose missions and powers are compatible with choice.[57]

In addition to state and local governments, private philanthropies and the federal government can contribute to the sensible design, implementation, evaluation, and refinement of choice programs. Philanthropy's potential role can be significant: in sponsoring planning for choice, developing the capacities of schools and educators, and providing a "watchdog" function, ensuring that someone complains if choice programs are not implemented as planned. (This function has proven indispensable in the implementation of other large-scale education reforms which, left entirely to school district politics, are seldom implemented as promised.)[58]

Though local government agencies might be able to perform all of the parent information, school support, and evaluation tasks implied by choice, some of these functions could be privately supported. Philanthropies in places like Chicago, Seattle, Portland, and Chattanooga have supported independent groups to provide public information and invest in new school capacity. Foundations and business philanthropies, including the Public Education Funds that exist in most big cities, can contribute a great deal toward successful phasing-in of choice.

Finally, though choice is largely a state and local matter, the federal government can facilitate transition, by allowing categorical program funds to follow children to new schools of choice and by investing in national research on how choice works.

Choice programs will not be implemented easily or even cheaply. The surest way to help guarantee their success will be conscious, well-thought-out strategies drawing on the best thinking of the worlds of government and philanthropy. And perhaps the surest way to encourage their failure is to implement choice programs quickly, carelessly, and cheaply, optimistic that at some point things will all work out for the best.

Conclusions

The policy issues and design tasks outlined above are challenging, but they are not really new. Standards-based reform, No Child Left Behind, and charter school laws require states and districts to think through many of the same dilemmas.

Communities can decide whether to make expansion of choice a conscious strategy, or they can let choice happen to them. Expanding choice implies that communities will provide some schools in new ways and also eliminate inequitable policies that plague district-run schools serving the poor. Doing new things well is not beyond human capacity, but it requires time, experience, and close analysis of what works and what does not.

Events in many ways may outrun plans, particularly as the choice elements of the new federal No Child Left Behind legislation become more salient. Families will continue to pursue schooling options, regardless of whether public funding and oversight are well-structured or poorly considered. If choice is not deliberately extended to those who now suffer because they don't have it, it will be extended nonetheless via private actions—private voucher programs, homeschooling, use of the Internet, growth of self-starting private schools, and the like. These actions may or may not benefit those who most need them, but if they develop haphazardly it will be more difficult to maintain a coherent system for educating the public's children.

Some believe that even careful, measured expansion of choice is a threat to public education. As this document makes clear, a lot depends on how communities and policymakers proceed. It is equally possible that, just as Franklin D. Roosevelt used the power of government to save capitalism from itself, current state and local leaders can employ the power of choice to improve their chances of achieving the great goals of public education.

APPENDICES

A.   Commission Prospectus

B.   Commission Papers

APPENDIX A

Commission Prospectus

Below is the initial prospectus under which the Commission proposed to work:

The problem: discourse on choice is driven by hopes and fears, not facts.

- Claims and counter claims are lurid
- Standards of evidence and definitions are unstable
- Data from "natural experiments" are subject to competing interpretations
- Unions duel with choice supporters via one-sided reports
- The contending parties have little incentive to ask the right questions or to agree on common ground

Choice is not an instructional program and its effects are conditional.

Today, the most best-known studies average out the effects of choice under very different circumstances. Such studies resolve little. Whether students who exercise choice benefit depends on factors current studies largely ignore:

- Who gets choice and who takes advantage of opportunities to choose
- Why parents choose
- The supply of good school options
- Whether parents can get information
- What schools families choose
- Whether students are well matched with the programs of chosen schools
- How well chosen schools adapt to children's needs

Other choice outcomes are similarly contingent:

- Consequences for students left behind depend on the behavior of their principals and teachers
- Consequences for schools left behind depend on actions of the school board
- Class or race segregation depends on who is eligible to choose and how schools admit students

Choice itself does not cause any outcome, good or bad. Everything depends on what happens next.

If we look inside the black box the most important questions can be answered.

It is much more productive to ask what determines whether choice leads to:

- Learning gains for children in chosen schools
- Improvements in the overall supply of schools
- Learning gains or losses for children in schools abandoned by choosers
- Widening or narrowing of the achievement gap
- Increases or decreases in student segregation by race or class
- Improvements or decrements in students' learning of democratic values
- Efficient or wasteful use of public funds
- Greater or lesser parental trust and satisfaction
- Increase or decrease in taxpayer support for K-12 education

These questions are susceptible to evidence and can be addressed empirically.

A National Working Commission could produce results people can use.

- Identify the real benefits and risks of choice under differing circumstances
- Suggest how risks and possible benefits can be estimated and compared for different groups of students, families, and communities
- Reveal ways in which the design of choice programs leads to more or less desirable results
- Propose research to clarify the connections between program design and outcomes for children, parents, and communities
- Help policymakers, educators, and parents make up their own minds

The fundamental work could be done in two years.

First year: Identify the outcomes of choice that are important to all the different constituencies. Understand the importance of:

- Availability of good school options
- Fair funding for all schools

- Information available to parents
- Effective regulation of school admissions
- Freedom for "schools left behind" to adapt their programs
- Resources to promote creation of new alternatives and improvement of existing schools

Then:
- Assess what is known about how these intervening factors can be controlled
- Identify localities that have promising supply-side, information, or regulatory programs
- Identify needs for new information and suggest or initiate studies

Second year: Formulate reports to inform policymakers, educators, and parents about what research now shows. Explain how choice works and how it can lead to positive and negative results:
- Show the range of ways in which choice programs can be designed; illustrate with local examples
- Advocate for the design and funding of studies and experiments required to address unresolved questions

Working Commission members would be people in search of answers.
- Respected thinkers and researchers
- People with differing views of choice but with open minds and time for serious work
- People with different analytical traditions including philosophy and law
- A diverse group in terms of ethnicity, region, and political affiliation

The Working Commission would produce a constant flow of information.
- Progress reports every six months
- Website and resource guides, first available at the end of twelve months
- Final report in book form and on the Internet
- Brookings Conference to explain and discuss the final report

Brookings' Brown Center provides a credible home and a national stage.
Brookings will:
- Convene and administer the Commission
- Provide venues for both working and public meetings
- Ensure constant review of work by technical experts
- Manage public information campaigns and final conference in second year

The Brookings Institution Press will:
- Supervise peer review of collected papers and final book
- Publish, advertise, and distribute Commission products

Work could start in fall 2001, end in late 2003
First Commission meeting in October 2001
Final report draft available for conference on choice, December 2003.

APPENDIX B

Commission Papers

(The Commission plans to edit and publish these papers separately.)

Julian R. Betts, "Does Economic Theory Hold Lessons on Why and How to Implement School Choice?"

Julian R. Betts, Dan Goldhaber, and Larry Rosenstock, "Supply Side Responses to Systems of School Choice."

Brian Gill, "School Choice and Integration: Conceptual Issues for Empirical Study."

Dan Goldhaber, Jeffrey Henig, Frederick M. Hess, and Janet Weiss with Kacey Guin, "Choice and Non-Choosers."

Frederick M. Hess and Tom Loveless, "Peering into the Black Box: What Evidence on Participants in School Choice Tells Us about the Large-Scale Effects of Reform."

Laura Hamilton, "School Choice in the Context of Standards-based Accountability."

Laura Hamilton with Kacey Guin, "The Demand Side of School Choice: Understanding How Families Choose Schools."

Jeffrey Henig, "School Choice and Public Responsibility: Will Movement Toward Choice Erode the Constituency for Public Responsibility to Educate America's Youth?"

Jean Kluver and Larry Rosenstock, "Choice and Diversity: Irreconcilable Differences?"

Karen Ross, "Competition v. Equity, The Impact of Public School Academies on Segregation in Michigan."

Charles Venegoni, "Re-reading Empirical Studies of the Effects of Choice on Civic Values."

Stephen Macedo and Patrick Wolf, "An Introduction to Educational Choice and Civic Values in Comparative Perspective."

Patrick Wolf, "School Choice and Civic Values in the U.S.: A Review of the Evidence."

ENDNOTES

1 Many of the Commission members' papers will be published in a collected volume. See Appendix B, p. 40, for a list of these papers.

2 No Child Left Behind, enacted in 2002, provides for consequences for failing schools, consequences that range from provision of technical assistance and counseling, through providing funds for parents to use to purchase tutoring services for their children, to enrollment in other public or private schools of the parents' choice.

3 See National Center for Education Statistics, *Condition of Education*, 2003, Table 27-2 (2003 [cited]); available from www.nces.gov/programs/coe/2003/section4/tables27_2.asp.

4 See The Education Commission of the States, *Issue Site: Magnet Schools Quick Facts* ([cited]); available from http://www.ecs.org/html/issue.asp?issueID=80.

5 See Jonathon Fox, "Sending Public School Students to Private School," *Policy Review*, no. 93 (1999). Daniel McGroatry, "The Little-Known Case of America's Largest School Choice Program," in *Rethinking Special Education for a New Century*, ed. Finn, Chester E. Jr., Andrew J. Rotherham, and Hokanson, Charles R. Jr. (Washington, D.C.: Fordham Foundation, 2001).

6 These are often called "open enrollment" systems. A public school choice program operating in Seattle is described elsewhere in this report.

7 Re. Cleveland see *Zelman V. Simmons-Harris*, 536 U.S. 639 (2002). Re. Milwaukee see *Jackson V. Benson*, 578 N.W. 2d 602 *cert. denied* 525 US 997 (1998).

8 See Center for Education Reform, *Charter School Highlights and Statistics* (Center for Education Reform, [cited]); available from http://www.edreform.com/pubs/chglance.htm.

9 See National Center on Education Statistics, *Homeschooling in the United States*, 1999 (2001 [cited]); available from http://www.nces.ed.gov/pubsearch/pubsinfo.asp?pubid=2001033.

10 Commission member Julian Betts has written a review paper on this topic, which will be included in the Commission's collected volume to be published in 2004.

11 For a more elaborate discussion of public oversight by a leading choice supporter see Terry M. Moe, "The Structure of School Choice," in *Choice with Equity*, ed. Paul T. Hill (Stanford, CA: Hoover Institution Press, 2002). p. 211.

12 *Zelman V. Simmons-Harris*.

13 Commission members Tom Loveless and Frederick Hess have reviewed the available evidence in a paper specially written for the Commission. It will be published in an edited volume of Commission papers in 2004.

14 John F. Witte, Troy D. Sterr, and Christopher A. Thorn, "Fifth Year Report, Milwaukee Parental Choice Program," (Madison, WI: University of Wisconsin-Madison, 1995).; Marc Schneider and Jack Buckley, "Making the Grade: Comparing D.C. Charter Schools to Other D.C. Public Schools," (Stony Brook, NY: SUNY-Stony Brook, 2002).See also Luis Benveniste, Martin Carnoy, and Richard Rothstein, *All Else Equal: Are Public and Private Schools Different?* (New York: RoutledgeFalmer, 2002).

15 For a balanced synthesis of research in this area see Brian P. Gill et al., *Rhetoric Versus Reality: What We Know and What We Need to Know About Vouchers and Charter Schools* (Santa Monica, CA: Rand Education, 2001). Another good and balanced review is Paul Teske and Marc Schneider, "What Research Can Tell Policy Makers About School Choice," *Journal of Policy Analysis and Management* 20, no. 4 (2001).

16 For studies of individual city voucher programs see, for example, Jay P. Greene, Paul E. Peterson, and Jiangtao Du, "School Choice in Milwaukee: A Randomized Experiment," in *Learning from School Choice*, ed. Paul E. Peterson and Bryan Hassel (Washington, D.C.: Brookings Institution Press, 1998); John F. Witte, *The Market Approach to Education: An Analysis of America's First Voucher Program* (Princeton, NJ: Princeton University Press, 2000); and Kim K. Metcalf et al., "Evaluation of the Cleveland Scholarship and Tutoring Program: 1998-2001," (Bloomington, IN: Indiana Center for Evaluation, 2003).

17 Good examples from an extensive literature on this topic include: William G. Howell et al., "Effects of School Vouchers on Student Test Scores," in *Charters, Vouchers, and Public Education*, ed. Paul E. Peterson and David E. Campbell (Washington, D.C.: Brookings Institution Press, 2001); John F. Witte, *The Market Approach to Education: An Analysis of America's First Voucher Program*; Cecilia E. Rouse, "Private School Vouchers and Student Achievement: An Evaluation of the Milwaukee Parental Choice Program," *Quarterly Journal of Economics* 113, no. 2 (1998); John F. Witte, "The Milwaukee Voucher Experiment," *Educational Evaluation and Policy Analysis* 20, no. 4 (1998); and William G. Howell et al., "School Vouchers: Results in Randomized Field Trials," in *The Economics of Education*, ed. Caroline M. Hoxby (Chicago: University of Chicago Press, 2003).

18 Alan B. Krueger and Pei Zhu, "Another Look at the New York City School Voucher Experiment," (2003).

19 John Barnard et al., "Principal Stratification Approach to Broken Randomized Experiments: A Case Study of School Choice Vouchers in New York City," *Journal of the American Statistical Association* 98, no. 462 (2003). For further commentary by education policy researchers see Paul E. Peterson and William G. Howell, "Efficiency, Bias, and Classification Schemes: Estimating Private-School Impact on Test Scores in the New York City Voucher Experiment," (Cambridge, MA: Harvard Program on Education Policy and Governance, 2003). See also David Myers, "Comments on 'Another Look at the New York City School Voucher Experiment,'" (Washington, D.C.: Mathematica Policy Research, 2003).

20 Tom Loveless, "How Well Are America's Students Learning?" in *The Brown Center Report on Education* (Washington, D.C.: Brookings Institution, 2002). See also Richard Buddin and Ron Zimmer, "Academic Outcomes," in *Charter School Operations and Performance: Evidence from California* (Santa Monica, CA: Rand Education, 2003).

21 Buddin and Zimmer, "Academic Outcomes." See also Jay P. Greene, Greg Forster, and Marcus A. Winters, "Apples to Apples: An Evaluation of Charter Schools Serving General Student Populations," (Center for Civic Innovation, Manhattan Institute for Policy Research, 2003).

22 Commission members Dan Goldhaber, Frederick Hess, Jeffrey Henig, and Janet Weiss, with the assistance of Kacey Guin, have written a review paper on this topic, which will be published in a collected volume of Commission papers in 2004.

23 Frederick Hess, *Revolution at the Margins: The Impact of Competition on Urban School Systems* (Washington, D.C.: Brookings Institution Press, 2002); Paul Teske et al., "Can Charter Schools Change Public Schools?" in *Charters, Vouchers, and Public Education*, ed. Paul E. Peterson and David E. Campbell (Washington, D.C.: Brookings Institution Press, 2001). See also Caroline M. Hoxby, "School Choice and School Productivity: Could School Choice Be a Tide That Lifts All Boats?" in *The Economics of School Choice*, ed. Caroline M. Hoxby (Chicago: University of Chicago Press, 2003) and Caroline M. Hoxby, "Does Competition among Public Schools Affect Parents and Taxpayers? Evidence from a Natural Experiment in School Districting," *American Economic Review* 90, no. 5 (2000).

24 Frederick Hess, Robert Maranto, and Scott Milliman, "Small Districts in Big Trouble: How Four Arizona School Systems Responded to Charter Competition," *Teachers College Record* 103, no. 6 (2001).

25 See Caroline M. Hoxby, "Introduction," in *The Economics of Education*, ed. Caroline M. Hoxby (Chicago: University of Chicago Press, 2003).

26 Caroline M. Hoxby, "How School Choice Affects the Achievement of Public School Students," in *Choice with Equity*, ed. Paul T. Hill (Stanford, CA: Hoover Institution Press, 2002).

27 Eric Bettinger, "The Effect of Charter Schools on Charter Students and Public Schools," (New York: National Center for the Study of Privatization in Education, 1999).

28 Edward B. Fiske and Helen F. Ladd, *When Schools Compete: A Cautionary Tale* (Washington, D.C.: Brookings Institution Press, 2000).

29 Two papers, one by Brian Gill and the other by Heather Ross, were written on this topic for the Commission. They will be published in an edited volume in 2004. For a strong statement of the possible links between choice and segregation see Amy Stuart Wells et al., "Charter Schools as Postmodern Paradox: Rethinking Social Stratification in an Age of Deregulated School Choice," *Harvard Educational Review* 69, no. 2 (1999).

30 Paul T. Hill and Kacey Guin, "Baselines for Assessment of Choice Programs," in *Choice with Equity*, ed. Paul T. Hill (Stanford, CA: Hoover Institution Press, 2002).

31 Jay P. Greene, "Civic Values in Public and Private Schools," in *Learning from School Choice*, ed. Paul E. Peterson and Bryan Hassel (Washington, D.C.: Brookings Institution Press, 1998).

32 Jay P. Greene and Nicole Mellow, "Integration Where It Counts: A Study of Racial Integration in Public and Private School Lunchrooms," *Texas Education Review* 1, no. 1 (2000).

33 See U.S. Department of Education, "The State of Charter Schools 2000, Fourth-Year Report," (2000 [cited]); available from http://www.ed.gov/pubs/charter4thyear/index.html. Nationally, white students make up 48% of the charter school population compared to 58% of the population served by conventional public schools. Charter school student populations are disproportionately white in Arizona, California, Colorado, and Georgia, and disproportionately minority in Florida, Massachusetts, Michigan, Minnesota, New Jersey, North Carolina, Pennsylvania, Texas, and Wisconsin, See also Casey D. Cobb and Gene V. Glass, "Ethnic Segregation in Arizona Charter Schools," *Educational Evaluation and Policy Analysis* 7, no. 1 (1999 [cited]); available from http://epaa.asu.edu/epaa/v7n1/.

34 Paul T. Hill and Robin J. Lake, *Charter Schools and Accountability in Public Education* (Washington, D.C.: Brookings Institution Press, 2002).

35 David E. Campbell, "Making Democratic Education Work," in *Charters, Vouchers, and Public Education*, ed. Paul E. Peterson and David E. Campbell (Washington, D.C.: Brookings Institution Press, 2001); in the same volume, Patrick J. Wolf et al., "Private Schooling and Political Tolerance."

36 David E. Campbell, "The Civic Side of Reform: How Do School Vouchers Affect Civic Education?," (2002).

37 Marc Schneider et al., "Institutional Arrangements and the Creation of Social Capital: The Effects of Public School Choice," *American Political Science Review* 99, no. 1 (1997).

38 Commission members Stephen Macedo, Patrick Wolf, and Charles Venegoni have written review papers on this topic, which will be published in the Commission's edited volume in 2004. In addition the Commission will publish a book of papers contributed by foreign scholars.

39 Choice might lead to increased segregation, assuming existing schools are extremely well integrated. It is much less likely to do so in large center cities where many schools are already totally segregated. Under choice, schools will need to make specific promises about the kinds of instruction, community experiences, and extracurricular activities they will provide, thus attracting some families more than others. That situation might lead to benign differences in student bodies according to individual preferences and student learning needs, but it might or might not lead to increased segregation by race or income. Much would depend on the kinds of schools offered.

40 Commission member Laura Hamilton and Kacey Guin have written a review paper on parents' use of information, which will be published in the collected volume of Commission papers in 2004.

41 Marc Schneider et al., "Shopping for Schools: In the Land of the Blind the One-Eyed Parent May Be Enough," *American Journal of Political Science* 42 (1998).

42 Commission member Laura Hamilton has written a review paper on this topic, which will be published in a collected volume of Commission papers in 2004.

43 See Hill and Lake, *Charter Schools and Accountability in Public Education*, ch. 7.

44 Greene, "Civic Values in Public and Private Schools."

45 See Schneider et al., "Shopping for Schools: In the Land of the Blind the One-Eyed Parent May Be Enough."

46 A number of scholars from different disciplines have show that choice helps construct mutual expectation and leverage between schools and families, which in turn influences student effort. See for example: James S. Coleman and Thomas Hoffer, *Public and Private High Schools: The Impact of Communities* (New York: Basic Books, 1987); Anthony S. Bryk and Barbara L. Schneider, *Trust in Schools: A Core Resource for Improvement* (New York: Russell Sage Foundation, 2002); Anthony S. Bryk, Valerie E. Lee, and Peter B. Holland, *Catholic Schools and the Common Good* (Cambridge, MA: Harvard University Press, 1993); Jacqueline Jordon Irvine and Michele Foster, *Growing up African American in Catholic Schools* (New York: Teachers College Press, 1996); and Paul T. Hill, "The Educational Consequences of Choice," *Phi Delta Kappan* 77, no. 10 (1996).

47 See Fred M. Newmann et al., "School Instructional Program Coherence: Benefits and Challenges," (Chicago: Consortium on Chicago School Research, 2001).

48 Commission members Dan Goldhaber, Julian Betts, and Larry Rosenstock have written a review paper on the supply side of choice, which will be published in a collected volume of Commission papers in 2004.

49 See, for example, Bryan Hassel, "The Charter-Voucher Connection: Learning About the Supply Side from Charter Schools," (Cambridge, MA: Harvard Program on Educational Policy and Governance, 2002).

50 Caroline M. Hoxby, "Would School Choice Change the Teaching Profession?," *Journal of Human Resources* 34, no. 4 (2002). See also Eric A. Hanushek and Steven G. Rivkin, "Does Public School Competition Affect Teacher Quality," in *The Economics of School Choice*, ed. Caroline M. Hoxby (Chicago: University of Chicago Press, 2003).

51 For a detailed discussion of how a moderately regulated choice scheme would work see Jacob A. Adams and Paul T. Hill, "A Regulated Market Model of Educational Accountability," (Seattle: Center on Reinventing Public Education, 2003).

52 Commission member Jeffrey Henig has written a review paper about the politics of local funding decisions, which will be published in a collected volume of Commission papers in 2004.

53 Other analysts have also made ambitious claims about what choice will cost. See, for example, Henry M. Levin, "Educational Vouchers: Effectiveness, Choice, and Costs," *Journal of Policy Analysis and Management* 17, no. 3 (1998).

54 This requirement challenges many local teacher collective bargaining agreements, which allow experienced teachers to avoid challenging schools.

55 Maguerite Roza and Karen Hawley Miles, "A New Look at Inequities in School Funding: A Presentation on the Resource Variations within Districts," (Seattle: Center on Reinventing Public Education, 2002).

56 See, for example, Kati Haycock, "Honor in the Boxcar: Equalizing Teacher Quality," in *Thinking K-16* (Washington, D.C.: The Education Trust, 2000); also Maguerite Roza and Paul T. Hill, "How Within-District Spending Inequities Help Some Schools to Fail," in *Brookings Papers on Education Policy*, 2004, ed. Diane Ravitch (Washington, D.C.: Brookings Institution Press, forthcoming).

57 A number of independent national groups have proposed such changes. See, for example, National Task Force on the Future of Urban Districts, "School Communities That Work," (Providence, RI: Annenberg Institute, 2002); Education Commission of the States, "Governing America's Schools: Changing the Rules," (Denver, CO: ECS, 1999); and Education Commission of the States, "Bending without Breaking: Improving Education Through Flexibility and Choice," (Denver, CO: ECS, 1996).

58 Frederick Hess, *Spinning Wheels* (Washington, D.C.: Brookings Institution Press, 1999). Paul T. Hill, James Harvey, and Christine Campbell, *It Takes a City: Getting Serious About Public School Reform* (Washington, D.C.: Brookings Institution Press, 2000).